Stress Less!
A Kid's Guide to Managing Emotions

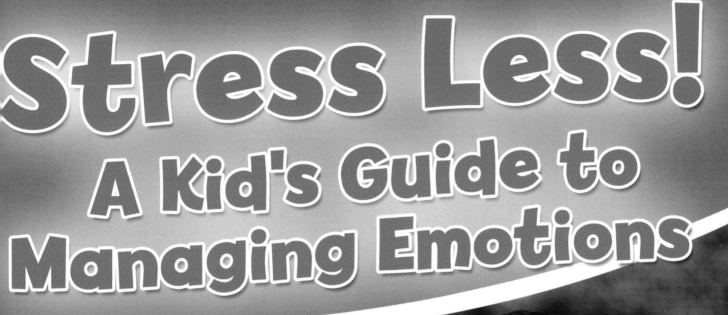

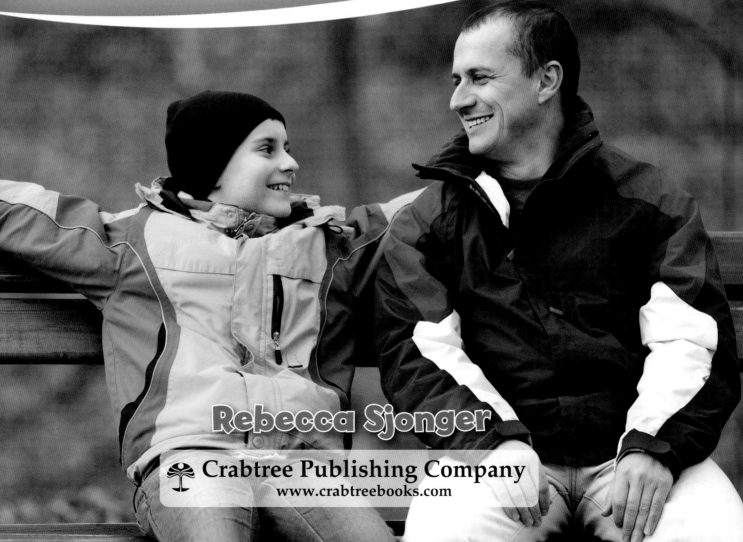

Rebecca Sjonger

🌲 Crabtree Publishing Company
www.crabtreebooks.com

Author
Rebecca Sjonger

Publishing plan research and development
Reagan Miller

Editor
Crystal Sikkens

Consultant
Steve Sanders, Ed.D.,
Professor, Early Childhood Physical Activity,
University of South Florida

Design
Samara Parent

Photo research
Samara Parent

**Production coordinator
and prepress technician**
Samara Parent

Print coordinator
Margaret Amy Salter

Photographs
arindambanerjee / Shutterstock.com: p. 22 (left)
istockphoto: p. 9 (bottom right), 18
SUSAN LEGGETT / Shutterstock.com: p. 7 (top right)
Thinkstock: p. 4, 5 (top), 9 (bottom), 10 (top 3), 11 (both),
 12, 15 (top 2), 16, 20
All other images by Shutterstock

Library and Archives Canada Cataloguing in Publication

Sjonger, Rebecca, author
 Stress less! : a kid's guide to managing emotions / Rebecca Sjonger.

(Healthy habits for a lifetime)
Includes index.
Issued in print and electronic formats.
ISBN 978-0-7787-1882-6 (bound).--ISBN 978-0-7787-1886-4 (paperback).--
ISBN 978-1-4271-1627-7 (pdf).--ISBN 978-1-4271-1623-9 (html)

 1. Stress management--Juvenile literature. 2. Stress management for
children--Juvenile literature. 3. Stress (Psychology)--Juvenile literature.
I. Title.

RA785.S56 2015   j155.9'042   C2015-903941-X
                                          C2015-903942-8

Library of Congress Cataloging-in-Publication Data

Sjonger, Rebecca.
 Stress less! : a kid's guide to managing emotions / Rebecca Sjonger.
   pages cm. -- (Healthy habits for a lifetime)
 Includes index.
 ISBN 978-0-7787-1882-6 (reinforced library binding) -- ISBN 978-0-7787-1886-4 (pbk.)
 -- ISBN 978-1-4271-1627-7 (electronic pdf) -- ISBN 978-1-4271-1623-9 (electronic html)
 1. Stress management--Juvenile literature. 2. Stress management for children--Juve-
nile literature. 3. Children--Health and hygiene--Juvenile literature. I. Title.
 RA785.S548 2016
 155.9'042083--dc23
                    2015021742

Crabtree Publishing Company

www.crabtreebooks.com   1-800-387-7650

Printed in Canada/102015/IH20150821

Published in Canada
Crabtree Publishing
616 Welland Ave.
St. Catharines, Ontario
L2M 5V6

Published in the United States
Crabtree Publishing
PMB 59051
350 Fifth Avenue, 59th Floor
New York, New York 10118

Published in the United Kingdom
Crabtree Publishing
Maritime House
Basin Road North, Hove
BN41 1WR

Published in Australia
Crabtree Publishing
3 Charles Street
Coburg North
VIC 3058

Contents

What is stress?

Does your heart pound before your sports team plays in a big game? Have you ever felt angry or unwell after fighting with a friend? Has worrying ever kept you awake at night? These are all signs of **stress**. Stress places extra pressure on your body and mind.

The signs of stress often go away on their own.

4

*One way to deal with stress is to **exercise**.*

It is normal to feel stress sometimes. Your family members, teachers, and friends have all felt stress. Each person reacts to it differently. This book will help you find ways to deal with stress.

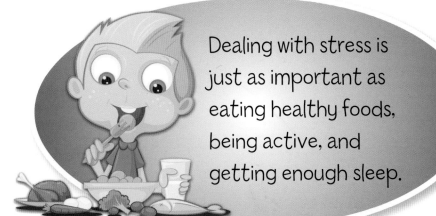

Dealing with stress is just as important as eating healthy foods, being active, and getting enough sleep.

Good and bad stress

Good stress comes from things you can control. Trying something new may be stressful, but it is also good for you. Stress over schoolwork can make you try harder. Bad stress is the result of something you cannot control. For example, being bullied or having a pet die can cause bad stress.

Can you find examples of good stress in the list below? How could stress be helpful in these cases?

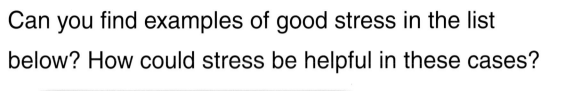

- ✔ **Doing homework**
- ✔ **Fighting with friends**
- ✔ **Competing in sports**
- ✔ **Moving to a new home**
- ✔ **Being a lead in a school play**
- ✔ **Family member getting sick or dying**
- ✔ **Starting a new grade**
- ✔ **Parents getting a divorce**
- ✔ **Performing in a recital**
- ✔ **Having a lot to do each day**
- ✔ **Seeing upsetting news stories on television**

How long does it last?

Remember that stressful times always end!

Most stress lasts for a very short time. It should end along with whatever caused it. Bad stress caused by an event that is out of your control may last longer. In some cases, this stress may carry on for weeks or even months.

Long-lasting stress may come from one big event, such as moving to a new town. When two or more stressful things happen at the same time, it may take longer for the signs of stress to go away. Stress that lasts a long time can harm your health if it is not dealt with.

If you are feeling sad, worried, or angry all the time, it is important to ask for help to find ways to deal with your stress.

Playing a musical instrument can help you relax and deal with stress.

Body signals

Your mind and body are connected. So, it is normal for your body to react in certain ways when your mind is under stress. A faster heartbeat is often the first sign of stress. You may also feel a quick rush of **energy**.

Other signs of stress might include sweating, dry mouth, upset stomach, headache, or cold hands.

Each person's body responds to stress in different ways. For example, you may not want to eat when you are under stress. However, your friend may crave food when he is stressed. Some kids get tired, but others are more alert and cannot sleep.

Tell a parent if stress is making you feel unwell.

11

Stress does not just affect your body, it also changes how you feel and behave. Good stress may make you feel eager or excited. Bad stress can cause you to feel angry or sad. The stress of having too much to do may flood you with many **emotions**.

You may have trouble paying attention or become forgetful under stress. Some kids become impatient or lash out at other people. Long-lasting stress may leave you with less energy. You may lose interest in activities you usually enjoy.

Pay attention to your feelings. Figure out why you feel the way you do. Is there a problem you need to solve in order to feel better?

Stress busters

Stress that lasts a long time can be bad for your health. Your body and mind may not function as they should. The next few pages include plenty of ways you can deal with stress.

Quietly focus on calm breathing and relaxing.

Listen to calming music.

Watch a funny video that makes you laugh.

Relax with a favorite hobby.

Write in a journal about how you feel.

Hang out with friends.

Plan ahead so you use your time wisely.

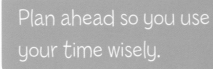

Go for a bike ride.

Spend time with a pet.

Talk about it

Talking about how you feel is a great way to deal with stress. Share your feelings with a person you trust. It could be a family member, friend, teacher, or coach. Someone who cares for you will want to help!

Explain what is causing your stress. Describe how it makes you feel. Ask for ideas that could take care of the problem or ease your stress. Knowing you have help will make you feel a lot better!

If you find it hard to talk about how you feel, you could draw a picture instead. Show it to someone and talk about what you drew.

It helps to talk with people who have also faced tough times. They will understand how you feel.

Healthy habits

Healthy **habits** help you deal with stress and your emotions. Junk foods and sugary sodas make you feel worse. Instead, eat **nutritious** meals and snacks. Half of what you eat each day should be vegetables and fruits. Your body needs plenty of water, too.

*Eat the rainbow! Foods that are different colors have different **nutrients** that your body needs to be healthy.*

18

Exercise helps improve your mood. Get your body moving! Go for a bike ride with your family, try a new sport, or jump rope with your friends. Aim for 60 minutes of activity each day. Getting plenty of rest at night helps restore your tired body and mind. Make sure you get at least 10 hours of sleep a night. It will help give you the energy you need to be active the next day.

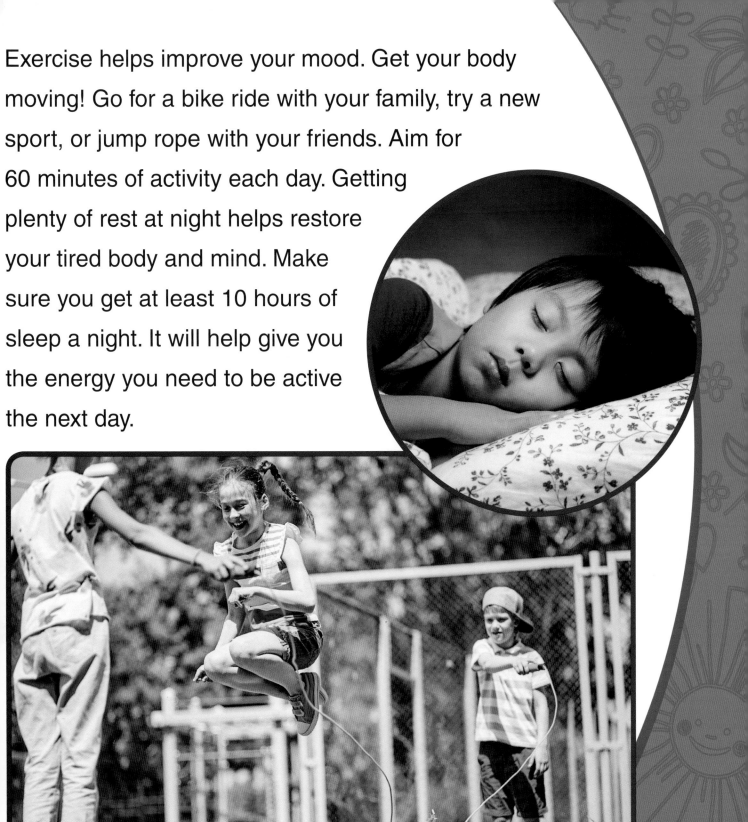

Breathe!

Did you know that the way you breathe can help you fight stress? Calm, slow breathing relaxes your muscles. It also slows down your mind. Practice the steps on the next page. You will then be ready to do them the next time you are stressed.

You can breathe like this anywhere and anytime you feel stress.

1. **Slowly breathe in through your nose as you count to four in your head. Imagine a balloon filling with air in your stomach.**
2. **Hold your breath as you count to two.**
3. **Slowly breathe out through your mouth as you count to four in your head. Imagine letting the air out of the pretend balloon in your stomach.**
4. **Count to three in your head.**
5. **Repeat the first four steps up to 10 times.**

Remember that stress is normal. It should not last long. If it does, talk with someone about it! What advice would you give to the kids in these situations? You can flip back through the book for ideas.

Raegan and her family are moving to a new city.

Jasmine is going to a birthday party where she only knows one person.

Ryan is nervous about riding a school bus for the first time.

Learning more

Websites

Find everything you wanted to know about feelings, including how to fight stress at:
http://kidshealth.org/kid/feeling/#cat20070

Got Butterflies? Find Out Why explains short-term and long-term stress.
www.cdc.gov/bam/life/butterflies.html

An activity booklet that includes worksheets to help kids deal with stress can be found at:
www.ag.ndsu.edu/pubs/yf/famsci/fs559.pdf

Books

Burstein, John. *Past Tense: Healthy Ways to Manage Stress*. Crabtree Publishing, 2010.

Donovan, Sandy. *Keep Your Cool! What You Should Know About Stress*. Lerner Publishing, 2008.

Schwartz, Heather E. *Stress Less: Your Guide to Managing Stress*. Capstone Press, 2012.

Most websites with addresses that end in ".org" or ".gov" have current information that you can trust.

Words to know

energy [EN-er-jee] noun The body or mind's ability to do work

emotions [ih-MOH-shuh-ns] noun Powerful feelings

exercise [EK-ser-sahyz] noun A fitness activity that moves the body

habits [HAB-itz] noun The ways someone usually acts or thinks

nutrients [NOO-tree-uh-nts] noun Parts of foods and drinks that help bodies grow and develop

nutritious [NEW-trish-ush] adjective Describes a food or drink that provides nutrients

stress [stres] noun The state of mind caused by strong feelings

A noun is a person, place, or thing.
An adjective tells us what something is like.

Index